I0339273

Something Something Morning

Chris Mason

© 2020 Blabbermouth Books

Baltimore

All rights reserved

ISBN 978-0-578-77838-9

blabbermouthbooksbaltimore@gmail.com

Cover Art: Ann Mason

for Ann and Elizabeth and Will

Contents

Of Us

For Ann

your politics Wobblie
surfacing probably
as authorities shabbily
think grabbily
and treat humans
like less
you notice this
and get furious

your posture wiggly
becoming giggly
during meetings boring
of pompous out-pouring
and suppressed snoring,
you sign
beneath the table
to other underlings
also wondering
"what for?" and
"no more"

more respected
to those selected
to be neglected
or rejected.
not suggesting
a fish thing smell
like a rose thing
nor proposing
changes in clothing

nor requiring
any rewiring

from **Where To From Out** (2012)

Acadia National Park
Mt. Desert Island
Coast of Maine

Mountainous
island surrounded
with tall waves.
10, climb boulders, arms
raised, ocean!
50, back here with
small family
and large family, eat,
walk, sing, bike
old black carriage roads
built by John
D. Rockefeller
Junior for
summering dancing
millionaires.
Forty-seven, fire
sweeps island,
hundreds of homes scorched,
island folk
evacuated,
mansions burn,
millionaires' parties
abandoned.
Mansions converted
to motels.
Fir and pine forests
grow back as
aspen and birch trees.
Folk move back.
Party, fifty-five

years married,
Mom and us kids and
our own kids,
arms on each others'
shoulders for
photograph, top of
highest peak,
Cadillac Mountain,
Dad looks out
past rocks waves past blurred
horizon
visitors and books,
backwards to
G.I. boat nearing
Belgium, World
War II, Dad's
friend on boat,
Roland, east coast kid,
Haverford
College, his mother
a beauty,
Dad, small-town book-worm,
wire glasses,
Roland, soon to die,
Belgium, puts
arm on Dad's shoulders,
pointing, "Look,
Gene, your first vision
of Europe!"

Deaf President Now Protest,
Gallaudet University,
Washington, D.C.,
1988

Deaf students pissed-off,
college picks
hearing woman next
president –
meetings, march, rumblings,
protests jam
campus; there among
students, Deaf
artist, Betty G.
Miller, her
paintings set around
her. "Ameslan
Prohibited": hands
chained, fingers
cut up, Deaf kids' mouths
puppet mouths:
"they want me learn talk
talk hear hear
like hearies – me try
hard equal
normal until me
freak fail why?"
Bass drum beats start each
down, Deaf school
football, loud low tone.
Thunder of
protest, lightning in
minds flickers
fingers in painting,

stories in
minds flicker – campus
all shut down,
all lit up – thunder
interprets
lightning: Gallaudet
President
I. King Jordan, Deaf.

Elsrode Ave
near Grindon
Baltimore

Elsrode curves
past cemetery -
Willy and
Elizabeth run,
touch carved stone
letters, stone fingers,
wings, baby
angel. Grave I, Ann,
and Willy
dug backyard old cat
Butter now
slight indentation
in grass where
matter has vanished.
New small cat
Ginger hides for weeks
inside of
Willy's storage cube.
Rupert says,
of Willy age two,
running full
speed through maze of aisles,
Normal's Books,
"Willy's got a plan."
Take 19
bus downtown, work tech,
arts high school,
stand, lighting cat-walk,
high above

actors, dancers, look
    down, hatch thoughts.

Gondwanaland Super-continent
Earth
450 million years ago

When Gondwanaland
drifted on
top of the South Pole,
end of the
Ordovician
Era, great
glaciers formed, sucking
water out
of Earth's oceans to
freeze and kill
many trilobite
species, sea
lilies, coral, clam-
like brachiopods
and bivalves - half
of all the
species on Earth. The
current mass
extinction being
caused by us
is happening so
slowly we
hardly notice it.
Two hundred
and fifty million
years from now
the continents will
merge again
into Pangaea
Ultima,

to be ruled by a
  great though now
obscure phylum of
  beings with
unlikely object-
  perceivers,
unthinkable thing-
  controllers,
and thoughts that do not
  seem like thoughts -
though even this is
  disputed
by scientists who
  stare outward
through human eyes, their
  thin fingers
typing frantically
  to name all
the creatures and all
  that they do.

Heimaey
Iceland
Edge of Europe

Eldfell Volcano
Island of
Heimaey, off Iceland,
erupted
Nineteen-Seventy-
Three, thousands
air-lifted, island
expanded
by twenty percent.
Walk around
island, sit, edge of cliff,
puffins fly
out over ocean,
catch fish, fly
back to humps of grass,
burrows, to
mates, sheep chewing grass
on sixty
degree angle hill -
Icelandic
book-remembering
folk, robbed bare
by bankers, let sheep
graze freely -
no sheep-theft worries,
only threat,
volcanoes and banks.

Kindergarden Room
Keewaydin Elementary School
Minneapolis, Minnesota

Cloakroom with jungle
gym size of
house. Big kid shows us
severed thumb
in box. Winter they
flood field make
rink. I sneak up on
gentle big
brother John skating
and push him
face first down on ice.
Teacher mad
sixth grade when we move
I don't thank
class for completing
my paper
mache yarn monkey.

Normals Books and Records
425 E. 31th St.
Baltimore
Maryland

Filling in
at register so
Rupert can
go to Post Office
see used book
just brought in – book of
my poems
I gave girl I liked
thirty years
back – inscribed "Ill-met
by moonlight
proud Titania".
Coffee stains,
finger-smudge, corners
of pages
curling, spine bloated
or spine cracked,
books sent out come back
older. The
flautist performing
at Normals
Books and Records, her
notes altered
electronically,
is daughter
of director of
J. S. Bach
Society my
mother in

Minneapolis
    sang Bach in,
their notes in moonlight
    now dispersed.
Each book on shelf at
    Normals once
lay open, face down,
    on someone's
stomach, half-asleep,
    half-mouthing
words just read to self.

Oberammergau,
Germany,
(Reenactment of Christ's Crucifixion)
Every 10th year

17, living
in Oxford
with parents, night brain
storm, knock on
bedroom door, their sweet
marital
embrace, open door,
shout, "Let's go
see the Passion Plays
this Spring at
Oberammergau!"

Pan American Highway,
The Americas

Dead Horse, Alaska,
(oil field town)
then meanders south
(but for one
undriveable stretch
rain forest)
to Tierra del
Fuego,
(site, petroleum
gas fields) home
of Jemmy Button,
abducted
by Darwin's Captain
Fitzhugh, brought
to England, new clothes,
learned English,
back with Darwin to
Tierra
del Fuego, met
Fuegans,
their language different,
finally
met good-looking girl,
wife, refused
trip back to England.
Taught a few
Fuegans English.
Darwin sailed
westward to flightless
cormorants,
giant tortoises

fucking to
bring variation
to species.
Name Jemmy Button's
mom gave him?
El'laparu. I,
high schooler
in England, hitch-hike
to Stonehenge.
Back, buy new release,
"Abbey Road":
bearded mop-tops cross
crosswalk, back
together, salute
the sun, then
split. Shipboard, Jemmy
Button would
tease Darwin about
sea-sickness:
"Poor, poor, fellow", but
when teased by
others, would cry, "Too
much skylark!"

Soudan Iron Mine
  Vermilion Iron Range
    Minnesota

Half a mile under
  Boundary
Waters canoeing
  area,
North Minnesota,
  abandoned
mine (no timbers, walls
  of iron),
The Cryogenic
  Dark Matter
Search – Geranium,
  Silicon
cooled down to one one-
  hundredth of
a degree above
  absolute
zero – see if hit
  by Weakly
Interacting Massive
  Particles,
raising temperature
  a little:
bits of dark matter.
  No hits yet.
Elevator up.
  Cool night air.
Some guys drink beer, see
  cosmic rays
making Northern Lights.
  Maybe those

muons are from that
    binary
star, Cygnus X-3,
    one guy thinks.

St Olaf College,
Northfield,
Minnesota

Grandfather Homer's
cheer: "Baseball,
football, swimming in
the tank, we
got money, we keep
it in the
bank: St. Olaf! It's
a college!"
Norse thought translated,
Homer's friend,
Kierkegaard scholar
Howard Hong,
"Diapsalmata":
(Either Or)
"What is a poet?"
(man roasted
inside metal bull,
flutes in bull's
nostrils make music
from man's moans).
College kid heard K's
dark words as
melancholy pure
elfish air:
Serotonin sounds
like snow sounds,
Diapsalmata.
Nord, Sud , Ost,
West, Heim Aller Best.
Hat, hat, head,

from, from, book, book, slide,
   sliding, down
snowy, St. Olaf
   Avenue
ice: It's a college!

Willits,
California,
1974

Hitchhike north Rt. 1
see Sam Rose
(Ellen Rosenberg)
craftswoman, dishroom
colleague, living in
refurbished
chicken-coop over
ocean, north
to Willits, teepee
home of Owl
Seagull, Ocelot
Real, poet
friends growing herb farm,
notebooks full
imagined and/or
Latin plant
name / pencil sketches –
well dry, they
move back to Berkeley,
study dream
therapy, tuning
pianos –
Joss later forest
ranger, Al
head, psychology
org, all of
California.   Drink
red beer near
redwoods, both deny
fact of that

red beer.   I and my
  brother John
ride trucks up hills to
  sky, down hills
to street, St. Vincent
  de Paul, San
Francisco, move old
  furniture,
new poems, daily
  minimum
wage hexameter.
  I, later
John, both move back East
  listen for
mouth of babes metric.

Xenophanes' Feet
Small gatherings
"Bounced around city to city"
Greek diaspora
6th century BCE

Rhapsode, singer of
Homer and
Hesiod for food,
also sang
strange 'silloi' against
all poets
and philosophers:
that Homer
and Hesiod's gods
stole too much,
screwed around, and lied,
that if cows
and horses had hands
they would draw
pictures of gods who
looked like cows
and horses, that clouds'
movements made
lightning (not Zeus, you
moron). Some
said Pythagoras
taught him. The
words Xenophanes
sung and beat
of staff to ground in
songs of new
science vibrated
inside ears

of sheep and shepherd
    folk and just
slightly rattled some
    fig tree leaves.
The aulete (flute girl)
    moving her
feet and fingers to
    X’s words
and beat of staff made
    guys go “Yeah!”

Yard and alley and garage and bushes
5109 29th Ave S.
Minneapolis, Minnesota
Saturday Morning, 1957

No time place equals
ecstatic
freedom of back yard
Saturday
morning in those place
times that have
back yards small kid can
go creeping
around by himself
or herself

Zooplanktal Cloud
Mouth of Blue Whale
The Living Ocean
The Barren Sea

Zooplankton, with
their eyes, brains,
shells, claws, antennae,
differ less
from phytoplankton,
green, photo-
synthesizing plants
and algae,
or nanoplankton,
cilia-
rich bacterial
drifters, than
from the far-submerged
residents
of Jupiter's moon
Europa,
percolating 'neath
layers of
ice in water warmed
by red hot
magma from deep-sea
vents like on
our earth life swam out
of. Blue Whale,
now decades older,
remembers
plankton eaten as
a young calf.
That was good plankton!

Voyager,
passing Europa,
elicits
no reaction. Hey,
life-ish stuff!
Icy heavens' warm
inklings, hey!

from **Wiwaxia** (2013)

Acrobatically

cat, hummingbird,

kid learning

to walk –

hand,

foot, x,

y, arms up,

king of sofa,

algebraical

Eohippian

cat-size dawn-horse

our tall horse

sprang forth

from:

Homo

Sapiens,

sing of noble

Eohippians

Heliocentric

Worlds of Sun Ra

composer

visions

of

versions

big band stomp

room spins we spin

hemoglobally

Inimitable

monkey snowflake

high lonesome

toddler

song

daughter

sang on lap

not froze on tape

illimitable

Medievalist

in the middle

of a dark

wood mid

life

middle

of winter

hears pure air’s chill

minimalism

Nether-transporter

Hermes leads souls

gibbering

down cliff

to

land of

dreams where all

souls survive as

neurotransmissions

Pharmaceutical

remembering

remedy

walk field

of

bees lift

forgotten

calves over fence

philosophically

Venerealist

fear, seventeen,

no sex yet

pimple

on

penis

ask Dad take

look, Dad looks, not

venerealish

Xylophonical

tuned bits of stuff

crash through haze

morning

step

traffic

let not harsh

xenophobes crush

xylophonium

from **Something Something Morning**

(2014 – 2015)

The Doik Man And Woman

When the dream said, "the doik
    man and the doik woman", right
after the bear scampered
    past me in the cave, friends in the
upper passageway having
    startled the bear, waking, I
wrote, "maybe 'doik' means 'made out of
    clay' as if 'doik' were more
subterranean than 'dink' or 'dork' or
    'dukie', the first
men and women fashioned out of clay
    by Sumerian
goddess Namma to do
    the dirty work down here on Earth

Radial Symmetry

Ours is era of bilateral symmetry,
        eyes, hands,
not era of radial symmetry,
        of starfish, five,
seven, or nine limbs, what if starfish
        were king?   Early chordate
pikaia, two inch long swimming
        worm-like creature with rod
down back supporting
        nerve cord, pikaia ancestor of
vertebrates, if all
        pikaias eaten by jellyfish,
starfish swimming, getting
        bigger, smarter, eating stuff up

Pocket Dial

Cell phone pocket dials daughter
            sleeping with boyfriend, pre-dawn.
Crickets, truck banging around, cell phone
            doesn't dial cranky
exuberant Mrs. Deener, or the
            bus driver
from Special Olympics.   My Dad is gone
            but still on the phone.
My sister found U. S. Savings Bonds
            grandparents sent us,
the note says, "We are proud of the
            young man you have become."
Hard to dial up the sound of their voices,
            even in dreams

Appalachian Banjo

The women's singing group
    in the forest is called "lightning",
also the name of the cake
    the singers had baked for their
sister's sixtieth birthday, recipe
    remembered from
mother who had years of forgetting
    after doing years
of oral history – children of
    missionaries had
become skeptics who ministered
    to souls they encountered
writing down their stories
    in the kitchens of the forest

Floating Fire

In the tub, accompanied

            by gravitons, neutrinos,

virtual photons and cricket songs,

            the water does not

penetrate my skin, repulsed by skin's

            electrical charge.

Nor does it penetrate my rectum

            which is closed.   In tub

my Mom cleans the ashes out of my hair

            from napkin I

held over candle, cousin's 10th

            birthday party, acting

on the older kids'

            experimental hypotheses

School

My student is mad he has to work and not
play with toys.
I am mad he is playing with toys not
working. I put
spreadsheet on his desk with spaces
for stickers. He throws it
on the floor. I say he can't
go outside unless he works.
He pouts. I fume. A great flock of birds
flies past the window
in a wide curve. Class runs to look.
The birds eat worms. The kids
look. The birds fly away.
Incidental learning takes place

First Job After College

The food investigator-facilitators
often
meet each other after work
for spaghetti and whiskey.
"If things are getting better," we say,
"then better ain't what it used
to be." The tiny typewriters
they give us come
out so smudged we
go over all the letters in ink pen.
"The smell of food among
the hungry is like a bugler
sounding reveille," we type
as the shipments get disbursed

Ears Perked Up

"I think I'd die of synaesthesia,"
John says, "if I was
eating Mom's fresh bread with melted
butter and you started
all that rattling and tapping."
One girl did this dance thing just
shifting her weight from left to right
for a whole hour.   The crowd
went wild.   That was during the
"Nuance" craze.   A group of us
would sit out there on the front porch
all night long just humming
until somebody's ex-girlfriend yells,
"I'm trying to sleep!"

Purplish In The Up

Stressed about learning to handle
all the new robots.
Grandpa said, on the boat, an older
robot gave him some
advice. "Don't ever stop
adjusting your hypotheses."
The sky purple, my middle
sensating, I longed for a
companion. My best friend's best
buds were disconnected
and she was languishing. "Extreme
consumption," Grandma would
say, "is adorable but
inevitably short-lived."

In Retrospect

Age twenty-three, I drove younger
sister Karen, twenty-
two, and brother Tom, sixteen,
to party. Tom and I smoked
pot, drank beer, fell asleep. Karen
mad, waiting hours for us
to wake up, drive home, but
doesn't remember it now. Tom,
sober twenty-six years, says I was a
bad example,
but it's okay. I stopped smoking pot
when kids got born, world
smoky enough, but son's friends
say I act like I'm on crack

Winged Song

At swimming pool, looking for
bass clarinet with which
to assess the students. The text: Hoagy
Carmichael. "Heart
and Soul." Sound of bay and air
at wildlife reserve peaceful
drone accompanies bicycle wheels
and honking geese. Some
geese said to have quit migrating,
plenty of corn on farm.
Others continue on, song sound of
dialogue with mate.
Erik Dolphy: "The notes are in the air."
A goose-eye view

Midnight Ramblers

In the club car of a train going
        nowhere I get an
earful from guy wants to cover
        whole frigging highway grid
with solar panels. I say it'd be
        cheaper to send
every blessed poor kid in
        America to Harvard,
all that brainpower walking the
        godforsaken streets with
a goddamn slide rule. We make
        a gentleman's wager, spit
in our palms before shaking hands
        as the train whistle shrieks

Phone Call From Uncle Jim

"It's just a pile of dirt" (U S A)

said some guy to Great-

Uncle Ivar, who almost fell off the

roof they were fixing.

"It's just a pile of words." (poem),

Jim to me, quoting dirt

story. Norwegian Zen

poetics from camp director

turned genealogist who hand-made

book about us kids,

"The Secret Treasure". We find

treasure box inside old tree.

In the box, nuts! Which we eat

and give to everybody.

from ***Matter*** (2017)

NICKEL

is
found
in
iron-
nickel
meteorites
nickel's
role
in
life
murky
some
enzymes
contain
nickel
which
arrived
Earth
in
meteorites
containing
silvery
white
metal

I
found
a
buffalo
Indian-
head
nickel
for
which
Cheyenne
Chief
Two
Moons
Calf
and
Lakota
Chief
Iron
Tail
served
as
models
for
buffalo

NICKEL

H_2O

hemisphere - of - humidity

heavens - open - heavily

handfuls - only - handfuls

helios - omnivorous - helios

hungrily - oak - humbly

hums - other - half-life

METHANE

plumes
emitted
from
cows
warming
air
of
Earth
whose
cows
emit
plumes
of

plumes
spotted
on
Mars
might
possibly
be
evidence
of
life
emitting
plumes
of

METHANE

CO_2

overflowering - crowds - overflowering

o’er - cumulus - o’er

of - centuries - of

o’er - cirrhus - o’er

out - carboniferousness - out

When

S H I T

quotes is
Wiki separated
quotes from
Henry eating
Miller by
who use
quotes of
Brazilian outhouse
folk infectious
proverb diseases
when plummet
shit yet
becomes poor
valuable farmers'
the poor
poor soil
will is
be nevertheless
born enriched
without by
assholes gifts
says of
proverb cows'
folk and
quote goats'
about precious

SHIT

O_2

orbs - ooze

origami - organelle

octopus - osprey

oceanarium - octogenarian

MOLYBDENUM

no
multi-cellular
life
without
trace
element
Molybdenum
early
evolution
multi-cellular
life
maybe
slowed
by
not
enough

at
center
of
nitrogen-
capturing
molecule
Molybdenum
helps
capture
Nitrogen
from
air
for
use
building
protein

MOLYBDENUM

<u>Some of the Methods of Performing Poetry Employed in and Around Baltimore from the Late 60's to the Early Teens by Poets in Their Late Teens to Early 60's</u>

(2013 , 2019)

Some of the Methods of Performing Poetry Employed in and Around Baltimore from the Late 60's to the Early Teens by Poets in Their Late Teens to Early 60's

David Franks jumping up onto a table to recite a poem, The Hopkins Writing Seminars, 1969;

Lauren Bender reading a poem from inside a large cardboard box, the i.e. reading series, Dionysus, 2007;

Blaster Al Ackerman reading a poem with a bar of soap in his mouth, The Shattered Wig, 14 Karat Cabaret, 2005;

Chris Batworth Ciattei reciting rhythmic blasts of images to thousands of grunge-rock fans, HFS-tival, RFK Stadium, 1992;

Marshall Reese picking a number from the phone book, reciting the number and reading a numbered poetic phrase for each digit of the phone number, Red Door Hall, the ailing Marshall Reese portrayed by Tentatively A Convenience, 1979;

Jocelyn Garlington reading lost family poem to percussion, sandwiched between dancers and comedy, Kuumba group, Café Park Plaza, 1983;

Ric Royer repeating each phrase of a poem 2, 3, 4 times, tonally modulating, Hamilton Arts Collective, 2009;

Bonnie Jones typing words to a poem being composed as it was typed and projected onto the wall, i.e. reading series, Clayton and Co., 2006;

Teen poet Clarence Robb of the defunct Baltimore Experimental High School spray-painting his one-word poem and moniker "CUBA" all over Baltimore, mid-eighties;

Bruce Jacobs reading a poem, accompanying himself on snare drum and alto sax simultaneously, the Litmore Poetry Library, reconverted church, 2012;

Chris Toll putting tiny books of poetry printed by Jamie Gaughran-Perez inside books at Borders and Barnes and Noble to be purchased unwittingly for free, 2005;

Lesser Gonzalez Alvarez shining 3-word poems hand-written in capital letters onto the wall with an old-fashioned educational overhead projector, WORMS, 2011;

Ellen Carter and Chris Mason reading mistranslations of poems by Paul Celan over the phone to surprised citizens plucked from the white pages, 1979;

Rod Smith exchanging chunks of poem for bursts of John Deiker's saxophone, in the basement, Madame Drogoul's 14 Karat Cabaret, 2011;

Afaa Michael Weaver improvising blues poems to blues banjo accompaniment, above the paint store, 1985;

Joe Cardarelli and Kirby Malone chanting strings of words through macrame masks, MICA, 1976;

Sharea Harris, singing the reading, reading the singing, dictionary and the uprising, City Lit, Inner Harbor, 2016;

Prison activist and poet David Eberhardt performing a rap for inmates at a barbecue in the yard, 2001;

Liz Downing, Mark Jickling, and Chris Mason singing poems of Sappho with banjo, guitar, and mandolin, Old Songs group, 2000's;

Adam Robinson, pasting poems onto walls around Baltimore, Is Reads project, 2006-2011;

Watercolorist and poet Richard Sober passing out free paintings at his poetry reading, Bread and Roses Collective Coffee House, 1978;

Animal rescue worker and poet Heather Fuller reciting names of dogs killed in dog-fighting matches, i.e. reading series, composer-reconstructed carriage house, 2009;

M Magnus performing choral Herakleitos in Dionysos, his daughter spinning from table to table spreading logos, 2007;

Lauren Bender performing David Franks' poem, "My Penis", as a redo, after David Franks performs "My Penis", i.e., 2006;

Joe Cardareli and Rupert Wondolowski and Michael Ball and David Beaudouin and Param Anand Singh performing the extended extemporaneous poetic introduction in whatever decades they landed in;

Some poet in a Baltimore row-house reading a love poem to a sweetheart who smiles in nervous bewilderment;

A poet walking alone on any street in Baltimore mumbling the lines of an unfinished poem, feet of the poet, feet of the poem;

Somebody reading poems in a strange tone of voice with funny gestures, whose name we forget and whose way of reading is too hard to describe, but it was great.

from **Daylight in the Swamps** (2015-2017)

12/31/15 (for Stephen Wiest: *Screeds*)

Poetry comes in the mail,

        written on an island.

As if words were birds

        seen from far away,

as if the shape

        of a cubic meter of ocean,

some part gravity,

        some parts wind, moon,

water's own viscosity,

        salty life,

some part

        Earth's rotation:

each word a wave

        that birds pass over.

2/6/16

8-year-old

hard-of-hearing girl in my

class from

El Salvador –

world's most

dangerous country says radio –

says Mom says

if police come

they will take

her and her 1-year-old

brother she is making

construction paper

birthday card for

during math class away

2/17/16

I eat more than my share of pizza.

     Easy to tell because

slices are fractions.

     We get more which is a mixed number,

harder to compare.

     I convert to fractions of

what makes me full,

     also a mixed number.

I have to shit but I can't,

     so I drink lots of water.

There's a drought so I

     go to two places.

There's a line to pee which sucks.

     Talk about karma!

2/22/16

Hopi Cultural Center

motel museum restaurant,

2nd Mesa,

50 miles drive from Tuba City,

Hopis we meet

eating supper, sunset vast mesa

seem like regular folk

but quieter.

Ann and I sit table

eat corn stew, fry bread,

my heart attack scare just

shoulder ache too much ipad,

Dad's death leftover panic:

2nd Mesa sunset supper

3/10/16

Principal observes lesson,

Performance-Based Evaluation System.

When Issa is three,

his mother dies.

"Motherless sparrow": kids are stunned.

Some of them same, some no father.

Computer freezes, no turn-and-talk,

points subtracted, principal leaves.

"Motherless sparrow,

come play

with me"

Kids write own haikus, earn

free time, run

helter-skelter round and round playground

3/12/16

"The words are in the air",

writes friend, signing

new poetry book.

24th birthday,

Anselm gives me his friend's book,

Alice Ordered Me

To Be Made.

Ann chanting

"Little lamb, who made thee"

to three-year-old Elizabeth,

who chants "All Fall Down!",

dancing around room holding book,

the words falling off the pages

into the air

3/21/16

Dream of tigers living

among us

like those raised by Buddhist monks

sweet to start

work week in city of

automobiles growling incessantly,

could take your life but

choose not to.

Pedestrians walk through

carnivorous traffic like

monks, challenging traffic's

materiality.

I steer metal beast with all my might,

to not hit thought-talking walker

4/25/16

Seven-year-old postcard Elizabeth

    wrote college music trip

Alba Italy to

    grandparents given to me

to mail, left in

    poetry book I

returned to library, it

    stayed on shelf, student poet

checked out book, found postcard, mailed it.

    My mother received it

seven years late.

    Dad not alive to read it.

Book that held postcard: <u>Miniatures</u>, Barbara Guest.

    Postcard-sized poems. "Love, Elizabeth"

5/6/16

"A human being is a

complex of . . ."

(Olson said "occasions"):

First year

Reagan administration,

girlfriend and I in

long skirts have

friends over,

attend Gender Fuck party,

fluidity

of gender debated sitting

in skirt on curb,

cool summer night behind

now defunct A and P

5/5/16

The sub-sub-librarian,
the collective bookstore
proprietor,
the junior pastor
of the left-wing church,
my mother,
my friend the post-punk
tattooed lawyer,
others who did or didn't
fall by the wayside
sing,
"Nothing nothing
nothing nothing,
talking 'bout the Monkey Man"

7/4/16

Six slender female
paleontologists
descend with ropes through
narrow chimney connecting
upper cave to lower chamber,
excavate bones possible
Homo Naledi individuals
walking with loved ones,
foraging, hunting, eating with gusto,
meeting tragic or long-expected
ends, bones ending up
mysteriously lower chamber to be
meticulously carried into sunlight by
six slender female paleontologists

10/9/16

Drop son off airport new home

    across continent L.A.

Winds whistling edge of

    hurricane Florida.

Airplane overhead not my

    son's airplane.

Loud sounds waking us at night not

    sounds waking son at night.

Football I throw not

    deep enough.

Notes son strums ukulele

    not loud enough.

Air carrying airplane shakes branches

    my limbic system my heart

10/14/16

Ann finds whitish oyster
        mushrooms, chanterelles, stringy
lions head mushrooms in woods, fried,
        delicious, for dinner, with rice.
Mom always said, "Eat your fungus".
        World's biggest organism
underground fungus. Plants have
        chemical signaling system.   Fungal
kingdom's path to dominion unknown maybe
        symbiosis – Unitarian lady grows
mushrooms basement sells basket farmers
        market to hippie couple fried up with
veggies, rice, spores enter nervous system,
        kids nicer but more inscrutable

12/30/16

Dream I spill glass of

water onto my mother's papers

on her desk. Everyone helps

clean up but can't

hide their displeasure. 'Displeasure'

comes from the root words

'disciple' and 'leisure'.

In the dream I rewrite the incident

using the term 'mouse-shitter' but

revise it again realizing

my kind father would never say,

"you little mouse-shitter"

to show displeasure at the spilling

of water on my mother's papers

2/12/17

Caps For Sale by Witislawa Zymborska.

When man sitting under tree falls
asleep, the hats stacked on his head
are stolen by monkeys in the tree.
A girl, covering the e - y with her
hand to show
the little word monk in monkey, sees
the monkeys as Buddhists.
"Buddhists do not steal hats,"
argues a boy. "Ancestral humans"
is her rejoinder, the man
divine or outer space. The caps being
caps of knowledge, the monkeys wisely
toss them to the ground

5/21/17

My brother and I each with
          loose teeth years dental
neglect, now brush better.
          I, insurance, he,
itinerant musician dependant
          dentists who help for cheap.
He worries false teeth change
          resonant vocal chamber,
I worry students laugh tooth gap.
          "Teeth worn out," sings Anakreon,
"charmed youth gone by."
          Our kind father, my teen years, holding
removable teeth, tip of tongue:
          awkwardly charmed supper-time teeth

6/1/2017

Radio relates Ket,

        remote Siberian language possible

cousin Native American languages, branching

        13 thousand years ago before crossing

Bering land bridge, similar

        word for 'people': 'dineh', deng'.

Word 'people' among

        cold Siberian tundra hunter-

gatherers and dry, arid, Navajo

        sheep-herders: dineh / deng.

Ask 88-year-old uncle what he

        does all day: "I talk to people."

My uncle talks to Deng.

        My Deng

6/12/17

The poem, a child of the 60's,
    is petulant and self-involved.
A character in the poem pees from
    inside his necktie onto the sidewalk.
The meter of the poem tries to be
    Jurassic but is only Cretaceous.
A critic says, "People are screaming
    out there," but says it petulantly.
The main idea of the poem is to
    emerge from petulance through
grandiosity into everydayedness.
    "You have become very everydayful, my friend,"
says the critic, his petulance
    having grown wings of grandiosity.

7/12/17

Drink cherry bitter beer

        friend's 40th birthday, cherries

antioxidant,

        cherry tree

chopped down for parking lot

        early childhood.

We teach students

        cherry tree honesty story,

Ann picks

        cherry tree leaves feed

caterpillar grow to

        Promethea moth.   Prometheus,

from rock, sees trees toppled,

        sacred forest lumber

8/16/17

5 wild turkeys, Minneapolis

backyard,

non-raptorous

national bird.

Ben Franklin,

slave-owner turned abolitionist,

kite lightning – ambient electric charge,

hemp-string, finger-kite, Leyden Jar.

Glass Harmonica, a friend in need,

early to, early to, bed, bed.

Musket perhaps but

jars of ionized fluids above fireplace.

Wild turkeys.

Early to, early to, lost time, rise

8/29/17

1898 Paul Laurence Dunbar

libretto: "Clarindy Or

The Origin Of The Cake Walk"

High-kick dance slaves make up mocking

slave-masters' minuets.

1908 Claude Debussy:

"Golliwog's Cake Walk".

1928 Clarence Williams:

"Cake-walkin' Babies From Home":

"Talk of the town – Teasin' brown –

Pickin 'em up – Layin' em' down".

Monk: "I lay it down.

You gotta pick it up."

Clarindy

9/16/17

Sun Ra's Arkestra, rehearsing
            at home
all day all night until
            all the visitors fall
asleep on the couch years after
            Sun Ra's body gives out, plays
Baltimore same day
            Cassini dives into Saturn's
atmosphere burning up so as not to
            accidentally land on
Titan or Enceladus,
            contaminating hypothesized
microbial life, its demise monitored
            by two-decades-old Cassini team

10/16/17

"What did your times leave our times, Dad?"
          "Smoky air and stinky water, Son."
"What did your times say to our times, Dad?"
          "Fix it your own selves you entitled brats."
"What did your time remember about
          past times, Dad?"
"Fun shit, like dropping t.v.'s off of roofs
          and watching them explode."
"How did your times pay for all of my times
          t.v.'s we exploded, Dad?"
"We sold a bunch of streams
          and bear eggs and some
equations and shit, Son."
          "I love you, Dad"

11/18/17

"Cat and Thou". Neighbor

builds cat house with

heater for

cat who peed on favorite

suit coat.

"Cat and Thou".

Cat licks my hair clean.

Cat brings us dead mouse gift.

Cats kill snakes,

ancient Egypt.

Cat on

radiator in sunlight.

Bug on window.

"Bug and Thou"

from **Thuslessness** (2018)

Thinkfulness

Dad, adult proponent of

reflective life, led 2nd grade

revolt against

"Given. Required. Work." on

math papers. Revolt,

joined only by

Whitlaw Lawson,

failed.

Mental math, inner chalkboard

many hands writing.

Irregardlessness

Notwithstanding

extreme greed's choke-hold on

this, this, this, and this,

semi-retired art-arborist

hobbles to soup kitchen,

ladles soup,

to river, sets up

river tower rock sculptures,

withstanding and regarding,

regarding and withstanding .

Stillness

Moth club lepidopterists in mountains,

dark night, no moon, hang

sheet on long string between

poles, light oil lamp behind sheet, see

hundreds of moths land, most

identified; tall, slender

teenage moth club girl,

moths landing upon

face, shoulders, hair,

still as a tree, feeling mothness.

Seeableness

Petroglyphs on boulder near river

visible only by boat;

cave paintings closed-up

cave visible

only on video;

words Willy scratched

with rock, hood Ann's new

car, age 4, car now junked,

"I love Mom", seeable

only on Ann's phone.

Frozableness

Pre-cancerous spots my
forehead and top of ear-lobe
made by sun, frozen
by Vietnamese doctor,
liquid nitrogen. "Your
forehead will
scare your students for
ten days," he says. Voice of
immigrant, old enough to listen for
bombs, memorize poems, 1960.

DelIcatessonlIness

Circus music friends serve

sandwiches to listeners,

each sandwich

unlike the others

as when

gorgeous red-haired actress

chews, swallows, with white wine,

fried insects of the orders

coleoptera and hymenoptera and

orthoptera and mantodea

My Spirographs (2020)

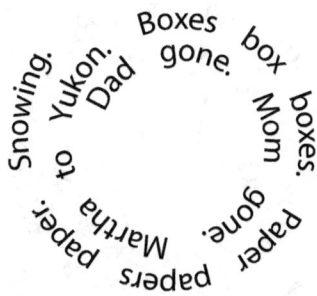

Dad gone. Mom gone. Martha to Yukon.
Snowing. Boxes box boxes. Paper papers paper.

Dad's Wittgenstein books, on shelf for decades, arrive used book store. Student buys, reads, at table. "The world is all that is the case." Ramen noodles. "The world is all that is the case."

Box of maps. Prehistoric voyages.
Humans arrive Australia on rafts. 10 foot tall flightless Dromornis bird.
2 ton marsupial furry Diprotodon. The Borrowers Afloat. Maps. The Borrowers Aloft.

Wooden clock given to teenage Tom deathbed of shop-teacher, ham-radio operator, wry bird enthusiast grandfather Homer. Turn of century wooden schoolhouse clock. Clock tick. Clock tick.

Martha's xylophone made from wood teach kids sing Orff method. Mallet wood Orff! Mallet mallet Orff! Orff!

Archivist Karen collates manilla folders family history. 1907 journal, 12-year-old farmboy Grandfather Homer: Playing ball, planting corn, finding bird eggs. "Had a little fun. Well I guess we did."

John finds my 11th grade Luther League youth service sermon in Bible in garage. "Celebrate the lives of the prostitutes! Celebrate the lives of the dope-pushers and the Viet Cong! For Jesus said, in Luke 6:32, 'If you love those who love you, what credit is it to you?' Celebrate the lives of the dirty, the ugly, and the repulsive." Unkempt, uncombed, no deodorant, Prince of Peace Lutheran Church, 1969.

John's high school newspaper story, The Magpies Come In June, Dear: John and Mary were young and in love. They were to be married in the Spring. One day, Mary said, „What if we were but characters in an author's story?" John cried, "But I can see, I can feel, I am alive!" Mary answered, „And what if he were suddenly to stop writing?"

Hmong wall-hanging of Laotian soldiers accosting Hmong family, embroidered blue and red thread. Hmong women planting Hmong plants Jim and Peggy's camp. Martha's Hmong students walking to school in snow.

John and Martha distribute librarian Mom's children's books to their own grandchildren. Minnesotan Wanda Gag draws millions of cats devouring each other, leaving one shy scraggly cat for the old man and the old woman to feed and adopt. Picture books recited, torn, taped, drawn on, given away. Wanda Gag, author of Gone Is Gone.

Drop off word-hive, dripping word-honey, Goodwill drop-off center, good word-hive, goodbye.
Peer squinting at centuries of usage through magnifying glass.
Two-volume Compact Oxford English Dictionary.

Dad plants 40 trees in 40 years, one five hundred millionth of trees needed halt planet's warming, enough for shade, birds, squirrels, forest-like air to breathe with and listen out for. Maple, maple, maple, maple, maple, maple, maple, woodpecker.

Mom's Fats Waller piano book.
Hears Fats Waller downtown Minneapolis teenager 1943.
Monday, Wednesday, Friday, eggs.
Tuesday, Thursday, oatmeal.
Sings, "The Joint Is Jumpin'," quiet house, age 93, November 2018.

5 siblings gathering, clean out parents' house. Small Tolstoy book. 23 Tales. "I have now understood that though it seems to men that they live by care for themselves, in truth it is love alone by which they live." To Agnes, from Gene and Joan, Christmas, 1949.

Of Us

One Day (for Rachel and Joe)

One
day at the
top of the world my
cousin Joe a teenage soil
scientist and his sister Rachel
a freshman anthropologist are given
a bag of seeds and a drink with the power to talk
so that everybody understands. Joe passes out the seeds and
they grow and make more seeds and everybody saves
the new seeds and passes them to the people
next in line and no one is hungry.
Then the semester is over and
a new brother and sister
team replaces
Rachel and
Joe.

Nostratic Eating Song

Muna[1] – madu[1]
munta[2] – matu[3]
eggs and honey
eggs and honey

Kusa[1] – marya[1]
coslo[4] – morya[5]
nuts and berries
nuts and berries

Zhugba[1] – paga[1]
zhumara[6] – piscis[7]
figs and fish
figs and fish

Tualo[1] – 'ala[1]
tiola[8] – alata[9]
stones burning
stones burning

Ema[1] – malga[1]

amma[10] – mala[11]

mother's milk

mother's milk

(All words found in and adapted from <u>The Nostratic Macrofamily and Linguistic</u> Palaeontology by Aaron Dolgoposky,1998).

Battery Battery Clutching Sunlight

1

Aluminum ions

water ions

ions of the air:

Flow electrons flow!

2

Potato ions

zinc ions

copper ions:

Jump electrons jump!

3

Lithium ions

Carbon dioxide ions:

Swarm electron cloud swarm!

Sky

North
Avenue
intersects Harford
Road near Circuit Court, mural,
painter Tom Miller, blue sky, yellow
sand, orange bird, African
man reading from book:
"However
Far
The Stream Flows
It Never Forgets
Its Source." Gobekli Tepe,
Turkey, giant granite slabs set up
twelve thousand years before now.
Carvings by hunter-
gatherers
of
snakes, lions,
spiders, cranes, vultures,
ducks, gazelles, geese, and people.
Blombsa Cave, South Africa. Rocks with
red ochre cross-hatch design,
seventy thousand
years old found
near
mollusk shell
beads colored with red
ochre, holes for stringing beads
together. Recess, Baltimore, 5th
graders who in class pick on
each other, hold one
another

up
on shoulders
like cheerleaders for
camera.   Deaf 5th-grade girl from
Honduras, her mom required to wear
a G.P.S. immigrant
ankle bracelet, paints
mural with
two
African-
American kids,
maybe boyfriend and girlfriend,
on ladders outside cafetería,
paint stars, moon, rocket, deep space
above where noisy
kids line for
lunch.
Daughter, then
age six, now grown, draws
picture story, keyboard near
window. Characters, Do, Re, Mi, Fa,
Sol, La, and Ti, stand to sing
on steps of treble
clef. Daughter
sings
their story,
keyboard my memory.
Orange and red leaves outside
dining room window drawn by the sun.

To Tom On The Farm

"And who the deuce can
parlez-vous a cow?"
Slide guitar arm slow
jam boogie in barn
to Facebook folks as
Corona bug swarms,
walking through fields of
corn, bread left on porch,
no touch, envelope
with check like milkman.
Forty years after
backing fake Elvis,
in North Dakota
North Minnesota
and South Dakota,
back to the Midwest.
Like Woody, Okie
in New York, lefty
in Oklahoma,
kids gather round, in
library or on
computer screen. This
guitar kills sadness.

St. Mary's College
Chamber Singers
"Dido and Aeneas"
Henry Purcell
(1659-1695)
4/23/09
Dir. Larry Vote

Like
Alcman's
7th
century
Spartan
girl-choir,
hearts
full
of
Aphrodite
and
Aphrodite's
son,
singing
to
crowds
of
bachelors,
these
student
singers,
hearts
full
of
Aphrodite

and
Aphrodite's
son,
sing
to
friends
and
admirers,
Purcell's
love-torn
Dido
and
God-haunted
Aeneas
through
forests
of
witchery
and
debauchery;
melancholy
solo
song,
raucous
ensemble
song.

Outside
night
air,
old
pond:
mighty
bass

bullfrog
choir;
from
dorm
radio:
“Talkin’
‘bout
my
generation”

Generations
of
kid
singers
sing
Henry
Purcell
who
died
before
he
got
old.

Old
pond.

Mighty
bass
bullfrog
choir.

for Dee-Dee, in memory P.Z.

Painter of zodiacal Nixon pics

Planner of xerographical scouting trips

Ponderer of xenophobic half-wits

Parser of the zen of hardships

Partner with Dee-Dee in zo-o-harmoniousness

Protector of the zone of serendipitous

Projector of zombie horror-flicks

Pointer at zebra-wisps

Peter Zahorecz

I. M. Michael Ball (1959 – 2015),
(Curator of i.e. reading series, 2005 – 2011)

Buying readers
          dinners
                    with
                              almost-existent money

                                        (*swarthy moom*)

                                        (*nuclear bugler*)

Helping friend scrape wall paper,
          prep to paint,
                    non-stop
                              poetics talk

                                        (*widget spawn*)

                                        (*bark stars*)

Drinking for jitters,
          introduction
                    of poets,
                              high-wire enthusiasm

                                        (*duck chums*)

                                        (*goramic billifuster*)

Supervisor, house-painters
          2008 crash,
                    laid-off, then
                              odd jobs only

(nuclear gnosis)

(local residue)

Back-pocket notepad,
hermetic sketches,
one day to paint
on small white boards

(fusky whence)

(twelve horizons)

No residence more than
six months – every roommate
turns
tyrannical

(my gnostrils)

(nomad stew)

Last apartment over
loud methadone clinic –
only heat hot-water pipes -
sleeping bag life

(frail lit)

(undulant skurf)

Sitting for hours,
sunny day,
self-rolled cigarettes,
shape of smoke ascending

(blent time)

(rowr aulx)

(Words in italics above excerpted from Michael Ball's poetry blog, "Mole Fizz").

Permafrost oh Permafrost
(for Nora Ligorano and Marshall Reese)

Permafrost oh Permafrost,
'Eskimo ice cream' defined by
Inuit NPR commentator as
mashed potatoes + blueberries
+ whale blubber

Permarost oh Permafrot,
Frozen Woolly Rhinoceros thaws to wonderment,
has odorous cloud

Permarost h Permafro,
Greenlandic singer Ole Kristiansen:
"Zoo and the people, zoo and the people,
I'm between the zoo and the people"

Prmarost h Permafro,
Nunavut Inuit homes' foundations cracking

Prmaost h Prmfro,
Thawing Przawalski horse has virus cloud

Prmaot h Prmfro,
Siberian train tracks twisted

Prmao h Pmfro,
Taiga spruce trees grow tilted
"Drunken Forest" phenomenon

Prmao Pmfr,
Batagaika Crater: thermokarst megaslump
depression Yakut people call

"Doorway to the Underworld"

Pmao Pmf,
Thawing Cave-lion carbon cloud

Pmao Pf,
Thawing Archaea methane cloud

Pmao Pf,
Ground akimbo

Pma f,

Pma f

Great Inventors

Hephaestus
Hephaestus is making 3-legged pots
with wheels on the legs.
They go wherever he tells them to go.
In Greek they are called "Automata".

Leonardo
Leonardo designs an ornithopter with
flapping mechanical bat-like wings but
the first guy falls off a wall onto his head.
Passers-by snicker, "Ornitottero!".

Somebody
Somebody is growing swarms of bacterial
solar cells, like blue-green algae,
for generating inexpensive current.
Pundits lampoon "Bio-foolishness".

A Bunch of Cows
A bunch of cows are farting. One of them
says, "Let's use our methane to heat houses
like the cow-pies pioneers burned."
In cow this is called "Moo".

A Colony of Spelunkers
A colony of spelunkers is running
wires from the mantle to
lightning rods in the troposphere.
"The nights are warm but the days are dark."

A Gentleman Entomologist
A gentleman entomologist pays us
10 cents for each hundred lightning bugs we catch
in gallon mayonnaise jars. They flicker in unison.
"It's the monarch man!"

Gilgamesh
Gilgamesh comes back from across the water
all disappointed about no immortality.
He tries to freeze himself but the ice keeps melting.
The gods yell, "Get a life!"

A Gang of us Kids
A gang of us kids gets tired of smelling gas
so we hook up old telephone wires to a tree
that is buffeted by the wind and the sun and the
rain. A town wag calls us "The Sustainables".

Supplies

1
Red powder
janitor's
cart soak up
puddle pee.

2
Starburst fruit
candy red
pink orange
test reward.

3
Socks and shoes
kid from warm
country to
walk in snow.

4
Charger for
kid's phone whose
home has no
good outlet.

5
Box cat food
kitten her
Dad gave her
is hungry.

6
Markers for
non-verbal
artist home
draw Manga.

7
Box apple
Cheerios
not plain oat
Cheerios.

8
Bird house kits
wants extra
for sister
no extra.

Photography

1
Leave old Sappho book
open to water-color poems
        outside overnight
to be photographed at dawn.

2
Disposable camera
left on dashboard during meteor storm
        has handprints
of Solar System.

3
Small girl in photograph with grandparents
on dock at lake
        holding their hands
got married Saturday in their absence.

4
35 millimeter cameras
around necks of
        family members at Mt. Rushmore,
1962.

5
Pictured in National Geographic,
Silver mine workers;
        gathering on Google,
Lithium and Yttrium miners.

6
Photobook of social situations
with social captions
            to teach social skills
where knowledge of other minds is weak.

7
Camera perches on top of mountain,
flies alongside migratory birds,
            clicking, chirping
f-stop,   f-stop,   f-stop,   f-stop.

8
Leave box Dad's notepads in garden;
leave box daughter's 3rd grade journals in tree-house;
            sunlight and chlorophyll permeate pages;
bring boxes inside.

Zeno - zero

Dad
told us
paradox
arrow never
hits target
goes half
then
three-fourths
seven – eighths
of way - always
more fractions
to pass.
We
get old
we forget
things but never
forget all
forget
half
three-fourths
seven - eighths
not forget all
things forget
all things
not.
Zeno
we know scarce
info of life;
of Dad's life
we know
half
five-eighths

seven - ninths
always is more
story more
info
but
never
remember
all of arrow
paradox
told us
Dad.

For Joan Shirley Overson Mason

If you read this thank
the off-duty librarian
who every day turned
a page of sunrise
in imagination's early eyes.

If you can snap your fingers,
sing hi de ho with the harmonist,
the bedside songstress,
who, laughter or tears,
deepened our listening ears.

If you keep an armful
of dreaming child asleep
in rocking chair tide,
remember a grandmother,
troubled grand-daughter peacefully beside.

If I can say I sit
gladly upon this
madly spinning earth today
not yet careening outwards,
thank her who made me this way.

Northfield Boy Makes Good

Bird-watching through pre-war binoculars,
different species disparate behaviors.

19-year-old European Front infantryman
took a bullet, Forest Hurtgen.

Stuck in a tent, pouring rain,
imagining another's pain.

Densely wooded plot, "Plant more trees!"
Extra oxygen enters Earth's breeze.

"DFL Brothers, DFL Sisters,
Amnesty To All Draft Resisters!"

Nails splicing lakeside deck,
errant hammer, "Aw . . . . . Heck!"

Racey Saab, seized up, no oil,
to negligent son, "Just a car, no big deal."

Kind words to clerks, strangers and neighbors,
mindful of others' labors.

"Christopher, you have to use your imagination
to understand another person's situation."

Hands and knees, harvesting chives,
imagining other lives.

For Martha
and Karen

1

Words written
in a dream
hard to put
pencil to
without a
flashlight like
rocks frozen
under a
deep blue lake
remembered
from a map
in a book
from childhood
read by your
mom who is
here also
at the end
of a long
dock reading
a book to
herself by
sun's lakelight
remembered
by flashlight
reading to
circle of
kids in a
library

or your two
sisters in
room next to
your and your
brother's room,
in bunkbeds,
flashlights on
library
books as your
mom reads to
your sisters
whose flashlights
are turned off
while she reads.

2

Our mother
riding on
horseback with
her sister
Audrey and
two teenage
boys from a
ranch a church
property
her Dad had
driven west
to inspect
staying for
one week but
chose not to
ride horse down
Nicollet

Avenue
as her boss
Sports Afield
magazine
requested.
Photo of
her milking
goat with her
sister-in-
law Peggy,
painting of
a goat by
Picasso
she saw in
South of France.
Pelicans,
eagles, red-
winged blackbirds,
seen at lake.
The dog they
had as kids
died. Many
hummingbirds,
but no cat
in her life.

3

Singing "My
Blue Heaven"
while brothers
and I strum,
correcting
notes we sing

gently, in
the twenties
listening,
living room,
parents sing
duets, same
decade "My
Blue Heaven"
was written.
She and friends,
the Yankee
Doodlettes,
sell war bonds
with snappy
harmonies.
Singing my
young daughter,
back seat, long
trip, to sleep.
Climbing five
painful steps
to living
room. "Don't Get
Around Much
Anymore,"
ninety-three
years old with
whispery
gusto. Sang
alto, her
daughter's and
neighbor's, and
fellow book
club members'

choir. They sing
Norwegian
hymn, “The Sun
Has Gone Down”.

Acknowledgments

Thanks to Christophe Casamassima of Furniture Press for publishing Where To From Out and to Phyllis Rosenzweig of Primary Writing Books for publishing Some of the Methods of Performing Poetry Employed in and Around Baltimore from the Late 60's to the Early Teens by Poets in Their Late Teens to Early 60's.
Thanks to Dan Cuddy of the *Loch Raven Review*, Richard Peabody of *Gargoyle*, Mark Jickling of *the Shakemore Book*, Param Anand Singh of *Worms Quarterly,* Michael Ball, Justin Sirois, Lauren Bender, and Jamie Gaughran Perez of *The I. E. Reader,* Jen Michalski, CarlaJean Valuzzi, and Fitz Fitzsimmons of *JMMW,* and Adam Robinson of *Everyday Genius* for publishing poems from this volume in their literary periodicals/ anthologies.
Thanks to Dan Carney for setting some of these poems to music.
Thanks to Bill Engstrand for accompanying some of these poems on bass at a reading at Normals.
Thanks to my late sister-in-law Beth Covington who sent me a hemp notebook in 2005 which got me writing poetry every day again after a long period of mostly writing songs.
Thanks to the following friends who read these poems and responded: David Beaudouin, Don Berger, Dan Carney, Bill Engstrand, Param Anand Singh, Terence Winch, Rupert Wondolowski.
Thanks to Robert Schreur for publishing advice.
Thanks to Charles Brohawn, Liz Downing, and Mark Jickling for performing songs with me. Thanks to Ellen Carter, M Magnus, and Marshall Reese for performing poems with me.
Thanks to my siblings, John, Karen, Martha, Tom for lifelong support, and to the memory of my parents, Gene and Joan.

Thanks to my wife Ann, my daughter Elizabeth, and my son Will for everything. RIP cat Ginger.

Notes

For Ann: My wife, Ann Covington Mason, sign language interpreter, artist, swimmer, mushroom-collector, butterfly and moth fosterer.
Acadia: Homer Eugene Mason (Gene) (1925 – 2012), my father, professor of philosophy at University of Minnesota for 43 years, carpenter, bird-watcher, citizen of Minnesota and the world.
Deaf President Now…: Betty G. Miller (1934 - 2012), "Mother of 'Deaf View/ Image Art'". Artist, educator, counselor. 'Ameslan' is a now rarely used synonym for ASL, American Sign Language.
Normals Books…: Rupert Wondolowski, poet, songwriter, editor of *Shattered Wig*, proprietor, Normals Books & Records, Cobbledy World. Flautist: Anne LaBerge, daughter of David LaBerge.
St. Olaf College: Homer Edgar Mason (1895 – 1972), industrial arts teacher, ham radio operator, gardener, carpenter, wit, my grandfather.
Willits: John Mason, my brother, poet, reporter, educator, author of *Fade To Prompt* (Tuumba, 1982).
Alan Siegel, author of *Dream Wisdom* (Celestial Arts, 2015).
Jocelyn Real, park ranger and park planner.
Wiwaxia – enigmatic fossil covered in carbonaceous scales and spines, from Cambrian period, early multi-celled animal.
Nethertransporter: *Odyssey*, book 24. Hermes bringing souls of Penelope's suitors to Hades.
Something Something Morning, Daylight in the Swamps, and **Thuslessness** were all written between 5:20 & 6:00 weekday mornings before work, weekends later.
Appalachian Banjo: Dream referencing my aunt Sarah Refo Mason (1930-2002), historian, musician, spirit of laughter and caring.
Floating Fire: Birthday party for my cousin, Tim Mason, playwright, novelist, libretticist, author of *The Darwin Affair (*Algonquin, 2019), whose mother, Myrtris, gently disposed of the floating napkin I set on fire.

Phone Call From Uncle Jim Jim Mason (1928 – 2017), camp director who brought families from Chicago and Mpls /St Paul to be out in nature, historian, bird-watcher, funniest person I have ever met.
Shit: Folk proverb in Henry Miller also in Gabriel Garcia Marquez.
Some of the Methods.... Selected books by writers named:
Phyllis Rosenzweig (publisher), *Girls* (Primary Writing, 2011).
David Franks (1942 – 2010), *Touch* (Red Wheel Barrow Press, 1965).
Lauren Bender, *Status Update vol 1* (with Stephanie Barber, 2019).
Blaster Al Ackerman (1939 - 2013), *Blaster: The Blaster Al Ackerman Omnibus*(Feh!, 1994).
Chris Batworth Ciattei, *Everything In Particular* (Shattered Wig, 1995).
Marshall Reese, *Writing* (pod books, 1980).
Tentatively A Convenience (with Alan Davies*) tENTATIVELY, aN iNTERVIEW (2017).*
Jocelyn Garlington, *Then and Now Poems* (Buzzard Beautiful Press, 2020).
Ric Royer, *She Saw Ghosts, He Saw Bodies* (Publishing Genius, 2010).
Bruce Jacobs *Race Manners: Navigating the Minefield Between Black and White Americans* (2011).
Bonnie Jones, *Gymnastics*, with Jeff Surak (Rat Route Bandcamp, 2020).
Chris Toll (1947 – 2012), *The Disinformation Phase* (Pub. Genius, 2011).
Lesser Gonzalez Alvarez, *My Drawing Sort of Looks Like You* (2010).
Jamie Gaughran Perez, *There Were Rivers Before There Were People* (Big Luck Books, 2016).
Rod Smith, *Deed* (Kuhl House, 2007).
Afaa Michael Weaver *Spirit Boxing* (Pitt Poetry Series, 2017).
Joe Cardarelli (1944 -1994),*The Maine Book* (Meeting Eyes Bindery, 2004).
Kirby Malone, *Phantom Pod* (with J Cardarelli and A Hollo, pod, 1977).
Sharea Harris, *Dictionary* (Asherah House, 2016)
David Eberhardt, *For All The Saints, A Protest Primer* (2017).
Liz Downing, Mark Jickling, Chris Mason, *Old Songs All Birds.*
Adam Robinson, *Adam Robison & Other Poems* (Narrow House, 2010).
Richard Sober, *Adjusting To The Light* (2012).

Heather Fuller, *Dick Cheney's Heart* (Edge, 2015).
M Magnus, *The Re-echoes* (Furniture, 2012).
Rupert Wondolowski, *The Origin of Paranoia as a Heated Mole Suit* (Publishing Genius, 2008).
Michael Ball (1959–2015), *the i. e. reader* (Narrow House, 2010).
David Beaudouin, *The American Night* (Blue Nude, 1992).
Param Anand Singh, *Yr Skull A Cathedral* (Publishing Genius, 2018)
12/31/15 Stephen Wiest: My college poetry teacher. His poetry is in *Gist of Origin* & *Screeds* (Odd Volumes, 2013).
3/10/16: Translation of Issa poem by Matthew Golub from *Cool Melons Turn To Frogs* (Lee and Low, 2004).
3/12/16: Anselm Hollo (1934 – 2013), great Finnish and American poet and translator who lived in Baltimore for several years. *Alice Ordered Me To Be Made* by the great poet, Alice Notley.
4/25/16 My daughter, Elizabeth Mason, cataloguer, librarian, pianist, singer.
5/5/16 This version of "Monkey Man' by Toots and the Maytalls included "nothing nothing nothing nothing" to indicate rests when taught to my Deaf students by visiting steel drum artist Kevin Martin.
5/6/16 Olson said "An American" rather than "A human being" but I think he would have been okay with human being too.
10/9/16 My son, Will Mason, filmmaker and writer.
12/30/16 Joan Shirley Overson Mason (1925 – 2018), my mother, librarian, pianist, singer, bird-watcher, "spiritual source of seven souls".
5/21/17 My brother, Tom Mason, songwriter and founder of the pirate band, "Tom Mason and The Blue Buccaneers".
11/18/17 Neighbor: Daniel Doty, lawyer, children's book store proprietor, my socially-distanced chess opponent during pandemic.
Thinkfulness: Whitlaw Lawson: Victor Larson.
Irregardlessness: Doug Retzler, photographer and documenter of Baltimore Arts, special effects maker for films, co-founder of Ad Hoc Fiasco, Art in Nature.
Delicatessonliness: Paul Margolis & John Shock of the Polkats & Stone Hill All-stars, musicians extraordinaire, play circus music in this dream, & provide sandwiches.

One Day….: My cousins, Joe Mason, professor of Geography at University of Wisconsin – Madison, and Rachel Mason, Senior Cultural Anthropologist for the National Park Service, Alaska Region, author of *Lost Villages of the Eastern Aleutians* (National Park Service, 2014).

Battery Battery,,,: "Better Batteries Charge Forward", *Science News* Jan. 2017.

Nostratic Eating Song

Nostratic is a hypothesized language (constructed by Aaron Dolgoposky and Vladislav Illich-Svitych), proposed ancestor to Altaic, Afroasiatic, Indo-European, Kartvelian, Uralic, and Dravidian Languages, imagined to have been spoken by some residents of Central Asia 13,000 years ago. The vocabulary has been written in a simplified form, rather than in the International Phonetic Alphabet, in order to make it readable as a poem. I apologize for simplifications and mistakes. Nostratic has been criticized for using the 'nos' prefix, signifying 'us', although its derivation does not include many of the world's languages, including Chinese and Southern African languages. Hopefully linguistic technology will in coming years make it possible to construct a hypothesized language ancestral to all spoken human languages, though this assumes that human language arose one time rather than several times and does not include sign languages.

Notes: Languages used or misused in this poem:

1. Nostratic 2. Tamil 3. Malayam 4. Celtic 5. Proto-Lapp
6. Gondi 7. Latin 8. Altaic 9. Jewish-Aramaic
10. Old High German 11. Cushitic

(All words found in *The Nostratic Macrofamily and Linguistic Palaeontology* by Aaron Dolgoposky, McDonald Institute, 1998).

Permafrost…: Marshall Reese, poet/performer and Nora Ligorano, painter/ book artist, have created a series of ice sculptures of words such as "The Future", "Democracy". This poem was written for the ice sculpture, "Truth", installed on Washington mall, Sept. 2018.

The chorus was inspired by the favorite poem of my father, a GI in World War II: "Carentan O Carentan" by Louis Simpson, which ends:

> Carentan O Carentan
> Before we met with you

We never yet had lost a man
Or known what death could do.

The process of subtraction I used was inspired by the great poet, my friend, Jackson MacLow (1922 – 2004) (his poem "Phone").

To Tom On The Farm: My brother Tom toured as a lead guitarist with an Elvis impersonator for a while after high school in the late '70s. Woody Guthrie had "This Machine Kills Fascists" written on his guitar.

For Dee-Dee, in memory P.Z.: Peter Zahorecz,(1966 - 2006) artist, curator, activist, thought-experimenter.

The form of this poem was inspired by a poem by Aram Saroyan:

My arms are warm
Aram Saroyan

I.M.Michael Ball: Michael Ball ran the i.e. reading series in Baltimore, for seven years, bringing great poets to town and enriching my poetic life. His own poems can be read at molefizz.wordpress.com.

For Martha and Karen: My sisters: Martha Joan Mason Miller, French horn player, music teacher, English as a second language teacher, outdoors-woman.

Karen Malinda Mason, first curator of the Iowa Women's History Archives, mandolin and ukulele player, limericist and memoirist.

www.ingramcontent.com/pod-product-compliance
Lightning Source LLC
Chambersburg PA
CBHW071400290426
44108CB00014B/1631
9780578778389